# YOU CAN HAVE IT ALL.

CHIMDI M. OHAHUNA

# DEDICATION

This book's dedication is in gratitude to Abba Father, who has never failed to restore His beloved of everything lost, and the devil has stolen. And, to every believer who is relentless in exercising the authority given us in Christ Jesus over the works of the adversary, the devil.

# CONTENTS


**INTRODUCTION** 1

**HOW TO PREVENT PREVENTABLE LOSSES.** 8

**SOURCE OF LOSSES.** 26

**WHAT IS SIN?** 31

**ENTREATING GOD FOR RESTORATION.** 57

# STEPS PROPELLED BY IMMATURITY.  73

# REPLACEMENT OF LOSSES.  83

# PROOFS OF RESTORATION.  92

# HOW GOD RESTORES.  109

# ENFORCING RESTITUTION.  121

# THE TRUTH TO KNOW.  139

# HOW IS A THIEF TO RESTITUTE?  144

# HOW TO MAKE THE DEVIL RESTITUTE.  156

YOU CAN HAVE IT ALL.

# INTRODUCTION

The word loss is not welcoming to a man, as no one wants to incur a loss nor does any man rejoice over the experience of a loss. By English definitions, the word "Loss" refers to the act or fact of being unable to keep or maintain something or someone, and the decrease in amount,

magnitude, value, or degree.

Also, loss refers to the partial or

complete deterioration or absence of a

physical capability or function, a

person or thing or an amount that is

lost, and failure to gain, win, obtain, or

utilize.

Hence, in this life loss

experiences come in many types and

varying magnitudes. A loss experience can be something relatively minor or a major occurrence. Whichever it is, it has a way of affecting the one who has suffered the loss to a certain degree. And, depending on his capability to respond rightly by the leading of God, he may be affected negatively or positively.

This book provides profound biblical truths on the subject of losses with practical procedures on how to respond to losses as a child of God for it to work out for your good. The Bible says in the book of Romans chapter 8 verse 28, "And we know that all things work together for good to them that love God, to them who are the called according to his purpose."

In addition, this book covers and answers the questions that every Christians seek to know. Questions such as;

✓ Can a believer in Christ experience loss(es)?

✓ What are the possible reasons for the experience of losses?

✓ Who/ what is responsible for losses in the life of a child of God?

✓ How can what has been stolen be gotten back?

This book will trigger every reader to fight back for all that has been stolen from your life and destiny till now.

YOU CAN HAVE IT ALL.

# HOW TO PREVENT PREVENTABLE LOSSES.

As we journey in life we experience losses once in a while, some as a result of our ignorance, carelessness or poor decisions while others as a result of theft. Whatever may be the reason for losses, God hates losses, and He is eager to ensure that we get back all we have ever lost.

God is bent on ensuring that we get back all we lost and He made provisions for this in the Bible. These provisions are encapsulated in two (2) words that mean the same thing. They are namely;

   i. Restoration

   ii. Restitution

Restore and Restitution have the same Hebrew word לם: shâlam, and it refers to the following;

● to be in a covenant of peace, be at peace, peaceful one (participle), one in covenant of peace (participle), to make peace with, to cause to be at peace, to live in peace, to be complete, be sound, to be complete, be finished, be ended, be uninjured, to complete, finish, to make safe, to make whole or good, restore, make compensation, to make good, pay, to requite, recompense, reward, to be performed, to be repaid, be requited, to complete, perform, and to make an end of.

Notwithstanding, for more clarity, we will use the English dictionary to explain both terms. The word "Restore" is defined as;

1. To give back (someone or something that was lost or taken): to return (someone or something)

2. To return (something) to an earlier or original condition by repairing it, cleaning it, etc.

The word "Restitution" is defined as;

1. The act of returning something that was lost or stolen to its owner.

2. Payment that is made to someone for damage, trouble, etc.

Although both words mean the same thing, they both apply to different situations. Therefore, let's consider the application of both words, Restoration, and Restitution, to draw the line of difference between the words. And, to establish the need to understand their applications concerning the person who restores and returns by use of analogy.

Therefore, in application let us consider the cases below;

## CASE 1 - RESTORATION

God restores to us what we lost due to our carelessness, ignorance, and sin.

# CASE 2 - RESTITUTION

The devil returns to us what he stole from us with interest because he is the thief.

Hence, by way of application, let us consider the following analogy.

## Analogy 1 : RESTORATION

A person lost $20,000 five (5) years ago as a result of his carelessness, ignorance, or sin that is, it was his fault. But, God gives him

back $20,000 this year. (Joel 2:25)

## Analogy 2 :RESTITUTION

A thief stole $20,000 from a

man five (5) years ago from his safe.

Thus, it was not his fault, and this year

God ensured that the thief paid him

back $100, 000, which now happens to

be the present-day equivalent of the

$20,000 that he stole from the man

five (5) years ago. That is the accrued

interest as a result of inflationary and economic trends.

Hence, whatever man lost due to sin or ignorance is restored to mankind, while the devil makes restitution for all he stole from mankind in their current values.

The scriptures cited below provide the understanding of restoration and restitution.

*And I will restore to you the years that the locust hath eaten, the cankerworm, and the caterpiller, and the palmerworm, my great army which I sent among you.*

Joel 2:25


*Men do not despise a thief, if he steal To satisfy his soul when he is hungry; But if he be found, he shall restore sevenfold; He shall give all the substance of his house.*

Proverbs 6:30-31

*And the LORD spake unto Moses, saying, If a soul sin, and commit a trespass against the LORD, and lie unto his neighbour in that which was delivered him to keep, or in fellowship, or in a thing taken away by violence, or hath deceived his neighbour; or have found that which was lost, and lieth concerning it, and sweareth falsely; in any of all these that a man doeth, sinning therein: then it shall be, because he hath sinned, and is guilty, that he shall restore that which he took violently away, or the*

*thing which he hath deceitfully*

*gotten, or that which was delivered*

*him to keep, or the lost thing which*

*he found, or all that about which he*

*hath sworn falsely; he shall even*

*restore it in the principal, and shall*

*add the fifth part more thereto, and*

*give it unto him to whom it*

*appertaineth, in the day of his*

*trespass offering.*

Leviticus 6:1-5

The objective of gaining the understanding of restoration and return in accordance with God's word is to empower believers to recover all. Therefore, examining the words RESTORATION, and RESTITUTION is necessary.

## RESTORATION

*And he said, A certain man had two sons: and the younger of them said to his father, Father, give me the portion of goods that falleth to me. And he divided unto them his living. And not many days after the younger son gathered all together, and took his journey into a far country, and there wasted his substance with riotous living. And when he had spent all, there arose a mighty famine in that land; and he began to be in want. And he went and joined himself to a citizen of that country; and he sent him into* his fields to feed swine. And he would fain have filled his belly with the husks that the swine did eat: and no man gave unto him. And when he came to himself, he said, How many hired servants of my father's have bread enough and to spare, and I perish with hunger! I will arise and go to my father, and will say unto him, Father, I have sinned against heaven, and before thee, and am no more worthy to be called thy son: make me as one of thy hired servants. And he arose, and came to his father. But when he *was yet a great way off, his father saw him, and had compassion, and ran, and fell on his neck, and kissed him. And the son said unto him, Father, I have sinned against heaven, and in thy sight, and am no more worthy to be called thy son. But the father said to his servants, Bring forth the best robe, and put it on him; and put a ring on his hand, and shoes on his feet: and bring hither the fatted calf, and kill it; and let us eat, and be merry: for this my son was dead, and is alive again; he was lost, and is found. And they began to be merry.*

Luke 15:11-24

Following the account of the prodigal son in the book of Luke chapter 15, and the prophecy in the book of Joel chapter 2, we realize that the need for restoration only comes when losses have been experienced due to carelessness, ignorance, and sin; and life lessons have been garnered.

**YOU CAN HAVE IT ALL.**

# SOURCE OF LOSSES

The words of God to the prophet Hosea reveal the root cause of losses in a child of God. The Bible says,

*O ISRAEL, return to the Lord your God, for you have stumbled and fallen, [visited by calamity] due to*

*your iniquity. Take with you words and return to the Lord. Say to Him, Take away all our iniquity; accept what is good and receive us graciously; so will we render [our thanks] as bullocks [to be sacrificed] and pay the confession of our lips. Assyria shall not save us; we will not ride upon horses, neither will we say any more to the work of our hands [idols], You are our gods. For in You [O Lord] the fatherless find love, pity, and mercy. I will heal their faithlessness; I will love them freely, for My anger is turned away from*

*[Israel]*

Hosea 14:1-4, Amplified Classic.

Turning away from God due to the practice of sin always results in losses. For the proper understanding of the book of Joel, it is expedient to study the book of Hosea because Hosea gave rise to Joel.

The study of the book of Hosea, reveals how God used prophet Hosea's marital experience to symbolically reveal to His people, the Israelites, how they had departed from God. God through his prophet offered them a call to repentance and called for them to return to Him. The scripture in Hosea 14 verse 1 says,

*"O Israel, return unto the LORD thy God; for thou hast fallen by thine iniquity".*

# YOU CAN HAVE IT ALL.

# WHAT IS SIN?

Most times when we hear the word sin, we think of all the bad actions and things that humans do on earth but, this understanding only limits the understanding of the nature, act, and subject of sin.

Let's consider two (2) Biblical definitions for sin.

1. Sin is doing anything without faith that is, doing something with doubt and unbelief.

*And he that doubteth is damned if he eat, because he eateth not of faith: for whatsoever is not of faith is sin.*

Romans 14:23.

As believers in Christ, if we must do anything it must originate and proceed from faith. Whatever it may be, if it is worth doing it must be done with and in faith. If we know we do not have the faith to do a particular thing it is better we do not do it because, if we do it in doubt, it is sin. In order words, whatever is done without a conviction of its approval by God (it does not spring from faith) is sinful.

Also, the scripture in the book of Romans reveals that faith comes to man via hearing and hearing the word of God.

*So then faith cometh by hearing, and*

*hearing by the word of God.*

Romans 10:17.

Therefore, this implies that we must only do things that the word of God tells us to do because only then can we have faith to do them. Also, it means that doing anything that is not in the word of God, and not an instruction from God is tantamount to working in doubt and unbelief. Such an act is a sin that makes a believer experience losses.

2. Sin means to fall below God's standard.

Part of the phrases used to explain "hamartia", the Greek word for sin is, "to miss the mark". Hence, there is a mark set by God for mankind to hit as we follow His lead and do His will.

Most of the time this mark is taught only from the perspective of Godly character, but we must know that God's mark is holistic and all-encompassing.

God has a mark for our prosperity it is holistic i.e spiritually, soul-wise, and physically. The book of 3 John 1 verse 2 puts it this way,

*"Beloved, I wish above all things that thou mayest prosper and be in health, even as thy soul prospereth".*

When we miss this mark that God has set for mankind to hit as we follow His lead and do His will, we sin and this makes us experience losses.

For example, God's will is for you to live in health. Yet, you have chosen to live in sickness by not taking care of your body- not eating well, taking dangerous substances, and using your body wrongly.

By living such a life, you are making the practice of sin, the sin resulting from destroying God's temple thus, you have missed the mark.

*What? know ye not that your body is the temple of the Holy Ghost which is in you, which ye have of God, and*

*ye are not your own?*

1Corinthians 6:19


*If any man defile the temple of God,*

*him shall God destroy; for the temple*

*of God is holy, which temple ye are.*

1Corinthians 3:17

# Does God want His child to experience losses or otherwise stated, is it God's will for His child to experience losses?

The scriptures in the book of Joel 2 verse 25, and John 10 verse 10 respectively, makes us understand that God is a restorer as such God hates losses. And, God hates when his children experience losses.

In essence, losses are against God's will for believers in Christ. Whenever a believer experience losses God feels deeply hurt and desires to restore him. Hence, God never wants the New Creation to incur losses.

In Eden, when Adam lost his dominion over the earth and all creatures on it by selling his dominion to the devil, God was deeply hurt; and this made Him curse the earth for Adam's sake and curse the devil.

The Bible says,

*And the LORD God said unto the serpent, Because thou hast done this, thou art cursed above all cattle, and above every beast of the field; upon thy belly shalt thou go, and dust shalt thou eat all the days of thy life: and I will put enmity between thee and the woman, and between thy seed and her seed; it shall bruise thy head, and thou shalt bruise his heel. Unto the woman he said, I will greatly multiply thy sorrow and thy conception; in sorrow thou shalt bring forth children; and thy desire shall be to thy husband, and he shall rule over thee. And unto Adam he said, Because thou hast hearkened unto the voice of thy wife, and hast eaten of the tree, of which I commanded thee, saying, Thou shalt not eat of it: cursed is the ground for thy sake; in sorrow shalt thou eat of it all the days of thy life;*

Genesis 3:14-17.

Nonetheless, God did not stop at cursing, He went ahead to restore this dominion to man through Christ Jesus. In the book of Luke chapter 10 verse 19 says,

*"Behold, I give to you power to tread on serpents and scorpions, and over all the power of the enemy: and nothing shall by any means hurt you"*.

However, ONLY those who receive Christ Jesus, God's great gift of salvation to mankind, as Lord and believe in Him can have the restoration of dominion as it was in the beginning.

## Can God allow losses outside His will to come to saints?

Sin is the cause of the curse and the reason for all losses outside the will of God.

The scriptures in Proverbs 26 verse 2 say,

*"As the bird by wandering, as the swallow by flying, so the curse causeless shall not come"*.

This verse cited above simply implies that without sin there will be no loss.

When a believer makes the practice of sin, via his action has also chosen to run away from God's cover. That is, he has rejected the Fatherhood of God via the practice of sin.

And, under these circumstances, God cannot do anything to prevent the erring believer from experiencing losses.

Put differently, through his action to make the practice of sin, the believer has (in a figurative term) tied God's hands, and made Him allow something against His will to come to the erring believer.

Thence, as believers in Christ we must all bear in mind the following truths;

✓ God cannot stop losses from coming to us when we live outside His will.

✓ Although, God cannot stop losses from coming to us when we make the practice of sin, He cannot make losses come to us either.

Therefore, there is no need for mankind to blame God. God IS NOT the cause of the loss a man

experiences, and God CANNOT punish

a man with losses.

The invasion of the locust,

caterpillar, and palmerworm (called

God's great army) in the book of Joel

chapter 2 also helps us understand this

revelation. Consequently, a child of

God avails himself to go through losses

by living in sin.

Also, the devil takes advantage of

this room provided for him by the

believer. Because of the room created by living in sin, the devil can make the believer experience losses by stealing from him.

The Bible says,

*The thief cometh not, but for to steal, and to kill, and to destroy: I am come that they might have life, and that they might have it more abundantly.*

John 10:10.

# How can we prevent losses?

1. Depend on God's grace and live by faith.

*...but the just shall live by his faith.*

Habbakuk 2:4b

*But that no man is justified by the law in the sight of God, it is evident: for,*

*The just shall live by faith.*

Galatians 3:11

*Now the just shall live by faith:*

Hebrews 10:38a

*For therein is the righteousness of God revealed from faith to faith: as it is written, The just shall live by faith.*

Romans 1:17

*But he giveth more grace. Wherefore he saith, God resisteth the proud, but giveth grace unto the humble.*

James 4:6

*But by the grace of God I am what I am: and his grace which was bestowed upon me was not in vain;*

*but I laboured more abundantly than*

*they all: yet not I, but the grace of God*

*which was with me.*

1 Corinthians 15:10

2. Be full of the Holy Spirit (that is, live and walk in the Spirit).

When a believer is full of the Holy Spirit, the believer is empowered and enabled to pass all the tests of Satan to make him sin.

The Bible says,

*And Jesus being full of the Holy Ghost returned from Jordan, and was led by the Spirit into the wilderness,*

Luke 4:1

Therefore, the fullness of the Holy Ghost was paramount to Jesus' forty days journey in the wilderness, and His victory over the devil all through His temptations.

3. Depend on the grace of God to serve and obey God.

*If they obey and serve him, they shall spend their days in prosperity, and their years in pleasures.*

Job 36:11

*Wherefore, receiving a kingdom that cannot be shaken, let us have grace, whereby we may offer service well-pleasing to God with reverence and awe:*

Hebrews 12:28, American Standard

Version.

# YOU CAN HAVE IT ALL.

# ENTREATING GOD FOR RESTORATION

The study on the book of Joel chapter 1 reveals that the Israelites were in a very bad situation, they had experienced losses in successions.

They were experiencing a chain reaction of problems which led to continuous losses. A situation in which, while a person is still crying over one loss, another loss arises.

The fourth verse of the book of Joel chapter 1 provides an illustration of this situation, the Bible says,

*"That which the palmerworm hath left hath the locust eaten, and that which the locust hath left hath the cankerworm eaten; and that which the cankerworm hath left hath the caterpillar eaten"*.

These successions of problems gradually transformed into economic famine, dryness, meltdown, and recession which resulted in sadness and mourning.

*"Lament like a virgin girded with sackcloth for the husband of her youth. The meal-offering and the drink-offering are cut off from the house of Jehovah; the priests, Jehovah's ministers, mourn. The field is laid waste, the land mourneth; for*

*the grain is destroyed, the new wine is dried up, the oil languisheth. Be confounded, O ye husbandmen, wail, O ye vinedressers, for the wheat and for the barley; for the harvest of the field is perished. The vine is withered, and the fig-tree languisheth; the pomegranate-tree, the palm-tree also, and the apple-tree, even all the trees of the field are withered: for joy is withered away from the sons of men."*

Joel 1:8-12, American Standard Version.

This situation was not particular to only the Israelites in the old time. In recent times, it is happening to nations, individuals, and some believers in Christ Jesus.

It is painful for God the Father to see and know that some saints live as though Jesus did not die and resurrect for the whole of mankind. Because they are experiencing continuous losses which ought not to be the case with the child of God.

Any loss that is not for the sake of God's kingdom is not of God, and not from God. Such should not be allowed to exist or persist because God hates losses. So when losses are incurred, they must be replaced.

God hates losses and hates when His children experience loss. Hence, as children of God we are also meant to hate losses, and prevent them as much as we can.

Despite this truth, as believers, we sometimes still experience a loss due to our human weaknesses. These weaknesses could manifest in different ways, some of which are;

1. Departing from God's will by doing our own will instead of the will of God.

And, as earlier mentioned departing from the will of God entails the following;

.• Not acting in faith.

• Derailing from the ways and instructions of God.

• Living in disobedience to God and His word.

2. Taking steps propelled by immaturity (for instance, the prodigal son).

3. Taking steps and making decisions without enquiring from and getting the leading of the Holy Spirit. That is, choosing to do things in Ignorance.

4. Departing from God's will by doing our own will instead of God's will.

The book of Hosea tells of how the Israelites had departed from God, and God called for them to return to Him via the prophet Hosea.

*O Israel, return unto the LORD thy God; for thou hast fallen by thine iniquity.*

Hosea 14:1

One definition of Sin is doing one's own will instead of God's will, and this is contrary to God's will. The first sin ever recorded in the Bible came as a result of Eve and Adam doing their own will instead of God's will.

*And when the woman saw that the tree was good for food, and that it was pleasant to the eyes, and a tree to be desired to make one wise, she took of the fruit thereof, and did eat, and gave also unto her husband with her; and he did eat.*

Genesis 3:6

The above verse reveals that it was all about the woman's desires and will. She chose her will instead of God's will; this is all that sin entails.

Sometimes, our will as children of God may not be bad but, it is not perfect. Only God's will is perfect, and only God's will can make us fulfilled in life.

*...........that ye may prove what is that good, and acceptable, and perfect, will of God.*

Romans 12:2b

*For I know the thoughts that I think toward you, saith the LORD, thoughts of peace, and not of evil, to give you an expected end.*

Jeremiah 29:11.

Consequently, when a believer habitually seek to please his flesh at the expense of God, the following happens also;

- The believer does not act in faith.

- The believer derails from the ways and instructions of God, and

- The believer lives in disobedience to God and His word.

So, when a child of God habitually acts in doubt, perverts, and disobeys God's word willfully, he makes the practice of sin.

As mentioned earlier, the practice of sin is what makes a believer experience losses just like Israel did experience losses in the time of the prophet Joel.

YOU CAN HAVE IT ALL.

# STEPS PROPELLED BY IMMATURITY

Having stated that some experiences of loss are due to human weaknesses, one of which is taking steps propelled by immaturity. It is therefore expedient for every believer in Christ to consider the need to continually grow into maturity.

A believer can demonstrate immaturity in diverse ways. The account of the prodigal son reveals how he demonstrated immaturity. The Bible says,

*And the younger of them said to his father, Father, give me the portion of goods that falleth to me.*

Luke 15:12

The display of immaturity by the prodigal son is seen in his request for the wealth he was not spiritually, mentally, and physically ready to manage. This is because;

i. He lived under his father's cover all his life getting his upkeep from him thus, never understood what great responsibility his father carried to raise him.

ii. He was not in charge of any part of his father's estates unlike his elder brother, who was in charge and saw no need to ask for his share.

*And he answering said to his father, Lo, these many years do I serve thee, neither transgressed I at any time thy commandment: and yet thou never gavest me a kid, that I might make merry with my friends:*

Luke 15:29

iii. He never knew what true freedom was, so he thought that living under the care of his father was bondage. This was why he traveled to a far country the moment he got his share.

*And not many days after the younger son gathered all together, and took his journey into a far country, and there wasted his substance with riotous living.*

Luke 15:13

iv. He thought that he knew how to run his life and business alone without the help, leadership, guidance, and supervision of his father.

v. He thought he could succeed better in business than his father and he wanted to prove this point.

vi. He felt that his father was too rigid, stingy, and archaic and did not want to enjoy the wealth he had.

vii. He was ignorant of his father's heart, intentions, vision, and love for him.

The parable of the prodigal son and his wealthy father is a picture of the child of God and His Father God.

As children of God, whenever we take decisions and steps with the above-mentioned premonitions we are bound to incur losses like the prodigal son.

Notwithstanding the weaknesses which may result in losses in our walk with God here on earth, it does not change the truth that God hates losses.

The hatred God has for losses is the reason for His provisions for the replacement of all we lose. And, God wants us to maximize this provision.

# YOU CAN HAVE IT ALL.

# REPLACEMENT OF LOSSES

The scriptures in Joel 2 verse 25 says,

*"And I will restore to you the years that the locust hath eaten, the cankerworm, and the caterpillar, and the palmerworm, my great army which I sent among you"*.

We must therefore bear in mind that only God can replace losses of any and every kind, and He does so by RESTORING.

## How can we get God to Restore us?

We get God to restore us by entreating the LORD.

# How can we Entreat God for our Restoration?

i. Cry unto God for Mercy.

*Gird yourselves, and lament, ye priests: howl, ye ministers of the altar: come, lie all night in sackcloth, ye ministers of my God: for the meat offering and the drink offering is withholden from the house of your God.*

Joel 1:13

*Let the priests, the ministers of the LORD, weep between the porch and the altar, and let them say, Spare thy people, O LORD, and give not thine heritage to reproach, that the heathen should rule over them: wherefore should they say among the people, Where is their God?*

Joel 2:17.

ii. Turn from your wicked ways i.e Repent from seeking and doing your own will.

*If my people, which are called by my name, shall humble themselves, and pray, and seek my face, and turn from their wicked ways; then will I hear from heaven, and will forgive their sin, and will heal their land.*

2 Chronicles 7:14

iii. Come back to yourself like the prodigal son.

*And when he came to himself, he said, How many hired servants of my father's have bread enough and to spare, and I perish with hunger!*

Luke 15:17

iv. Come back to God like the prodigal son.

*I will arise and go to my father, and will say to him, Father, I have sinned against heaven, and before thee,*

Luke 15:18

Let go of pride and rise above the shame of what people will say and think to return to The Father through Christ Jesus. Recognize your wrongs and confess them and repent from all sins.

There is no better place outside of Christ that can be compared to Kingdom of God.The blessedness of abiding in Christ is holistic. Come back to God!

# PROOFS OF

# RESTORATION

The first proof of restoration is that the child of God takes the steps required to entreat God for restoration. The reason for this is that, although God knows our needs, He only supplies for or meets them when we ask Him to.

The Bible says,

*(For after all these things do the Gentiles seek:) for your heavenly*

*Father knoweth that ye have need of*

*all these things.*

Matthew 6:32.


*"Ask, and it shall be given you; seek,*

*and ye shall find; knock, and it shall*

*be opened unto you:"*

Matthew 7:7


Considering the account of the

prodigal son, we understand that

coming back to oneself or senses is

what precedes entreating God for mercy.

Before the prodigal son was restored in the book of Luke chapter 15 verse 17, says;


*And when he came to himself, he said, How many hired servants of my father's have bread enough and to spare, and I perish with hunger!*

(KJV)

Other versions render it thus;

*But when he came to his senses he said, 'How many of my father's hired workers have food enough to spare, but here I am dying from hunger!*
(New English Translation)

*"Then the son began to think about what he had done. He said to himself, "My father has many servants, and they have plenty of food to eat. They*

*even have more food than they need. But I will die here because I do not have any food."*

(Easy English Bible)

*"Humiliated, the son finally realized what he was doing, and he thought, 'There are many workers at my father's house who have all the food they want with plenty to spare. They lack nothing. Why am I here dying of hunger, feeding these pigs and eating their slop?*

(The Passion Translation)

These, therefore, reveal that the coming back to oneself or senses is proof of the mercy of God on that person. This shows that the person was not left by God all along nor was he allowed to be destroyed for his foolishness and rebellion.

Since the Bible says that the prodigal son came back to his senses,

It implies that he lost his senses when he lived riotously and in poverty. The sense he lost was the sense of sonship.

This is because no son of a rich father in his true sense will choose to suffer hunger and poverty when he knows he can go back to his father. It is exactly what has happened to sinners due to the fall of Adam and the same happens to Christians who chose to live as habitual sinners.

The prodigal son was still called a son even though he acted wrongly. Hence, his status did not change that is, he was still a son although now wasteful and extravagant.

So, although his lifestyle changed, His status remained the same. Right from when he asked his father for his portion of wealth, to when he traveled and spent the wealth portioned to him riotously, and till the moment he finally came back home to his father.

What then is the application of this truth to those who willfully act wrongly like the prodigal son?

Let us consider its application to the life of an unbeliever and to that of a believer in Christ.

## To the Unbeliever:

Due to sin, Adam fell from grace and this made him lose his sense and status of sonship and his lifestyle was changed from holiness to unholiness, prosperity to poverty.

Although Adam lost His sense and status of sonship, God did not stop seeing Adam as His son. We see this truth in the gospel of Luke in the listing of the genealogy of Jesus.

In the book of Luke chapter 3, the scripture shows that Adam is called "the son of God".

*which was the son of Adam, which was the son of God.*

Luke 3:38

Although, God saw Adam as his son, that did not automatically impute or impose the status, privileges, and rights of sonship on him.

Adam lost them due to sin, and by so doing he rejected the fatherhood of God over him.

Also, it was never mentioned that Adam come back to God to get them restored to him. God does not and cannot force His fatherhood on man although, He created man.

Man still has a choice to either make God his Father or not. The unsaved sinner is in the same situations and conditions as Adam after His fall.

Thus, everything applicable to Adam after his fall applies to the unsaved sinner.

In order for the sinner to be restored, all he needs to do is to come back to his senses and come back to God.

The hands of God are wide open to receive him and restore all he loses. God still sees the sinner as His son, and God earnestly awaits the sinner to return to Him to be restored.

## To Believers:

As children of God, our status does not change before God when we change our lifestyle from holiness to sin. God still sees us as His sons but, this makes us live below His standard.

When we habitually sin we expose ourselves to pains, suffering, poverty, and losses. All the believer must do is to come back to his senses and come back to God.

The hands  of God are wide open to receive the believer who erred and restore every loss.

YOU CAN HAVE IT ALL.

# HOW GOD RESTORES

From scriptures, we understand that God does not restore time but, God only restores years.

Page 108

*And I will restore to you the years*

*that the locust hath eaten, the*

*cankerworm, and the caterpillar, and*

*the palmerworm, my great army*

*which I sent among you.*

Joel 2:25

When the believer loses time,

God does not restore the time we lose

because God does not live and operate

in time. God lives and operates in eternity where time does not exist.

In the book of 2 Peter chapter 3 reveals that a thousand years is like a day to God.

*But, beloved, be not ignorant of this one thing, that one day is with the Lord as a thousand years, and a thousand years as one day.*

2 Peter 3:8

God created light on the earth, scriptures say,

*"And God said, Let there be light: and there was light".*

Genesis 1:3

This light God created was the light He lived in before creation, and the same light God lives in till eternity. That is why there is no darkness (night) in heaven.

*And there shall be no night there; and they need no candle, neither light of the sun; for the Lord God giveth them light: and they shall reign for ever and ever.*

Revelation 22:5

Hinged on this truth, we understand that Light has no end, and light is eternity. Also, the light God created in Genesis 1 verse 3 is not the Sun, Genesis 1 verse 16 reveals that God created two (2) great lights, the greater light that is, the Sun(light) to rule the day, and the lesser light that is, the moon(light) to rule the night.

*And God made two great lights; the greater light to rule the day, and the lesser light to rule the night: ...*

Genesis 1:16

The creation and separation of the Sun (day) and the Moon (night) is called TIME (that is,

Seasons/Appointed time). And, these occurrences only exist on earth.

*And God said, Let there be lights in the firmament of the heaven to divide the day from the night; and let them be for signs, and for seasons, and for days, and years:*

Genesis 1:14

Hence, God is not bound by time so He is not obligated to restore time.

Since a thousand years to us is as a day
to God, God restores us in His day
which is our years.

When God restores a man in His
day, He compresses all the man has
lost in years; and gives them back to
the man AT ONCE. Just as it was with
the prodigal son at his return.

Going by the account on the
prodigal son, we discover how in one

day the father restored the son for all he lost in years, this is the way God restores His child.

The Bible says,

*"But the father said to his servants, Bring forth the best robe, and put it on him; and put a ring on his hand, and shoes on his feet: And bring hither the fatted calf, and kill it; and let us eat, and be merry:"*

## Luke 15:22-23

Therefore, this account tells us that when God restores He;

- Makes whole or good something that was broken or reduced.

- Makes compensation for something that is damaged.

- Makes up for the damage, trouble, or something that was lost or stolen.

# YOU CAN HAVE IT ALL.

# ENFORCING

# RESTITUTION

As stated in an earlier chapter,

restitution comes in when something

was stolen from you, and it entails the thief returning or restoring to you the current value of what he stole. This entails paying the principal with interest.

The Bible tells us in the book of John chapter 10 verse 10 that, Jesus is the one who gives life more abundantly, and by implication, the devil is the thief.

*The thief cometh not, but for to steal, and to kill, and to destroy: I am come that they might have life, and that they might have it more abundantly.*

John 10:10

Every act of stealing is perpetuated by the devil,  and every human thief is his instrument or agent. This implies that thieves do not steal on their own accord or will; they are possessed, influenced, controlled, or manipulated by the devil perpetrate

such an act.

The devil makes a human agent

of his steal via the following means;

- Through the feeling of hunger.

- Through the need and desire to

survive.

- Through habit/ constant practice.

The devil makes his human

agent(s) start with stealing to end their

hunger or lack. Thereafter, it

progresses to stealing for daily survival and finally becomes habitual stealing.

Whatever reasons an agent of the devil has to steal, it is a deception given to him/her by the devil to make him/her steal.

God hates the act of stealing and also hates when His children have the experience of theft. So, God instituted ways in which a thief must restitute when he steals.

The following scriptures stated below are given to reveal this truth to the believer;

*"If a man shall steal an ox, or a sheep, and kill it, or sell it; he shall restore five oxen for an ox, and four sheep for a sheep...If the theft be certainly found in his hand alive, whether it be ox, or ass, or sheep; he shall restore double.*

*If a man shall cause a field or vineyard to be eaten, and shall put in* his beast, and shall feed in another man's field; of the best of his own field, and of the best of his own vineyard, shall he make restitution. If fire break out, and catch in thorns, so that the stacks of corn, or the standing corn, or the field, be consumed therewith; he that kindled the fire shall surely make restitution. If a man shall deliver unto his neighbour money or stuff to keep, and it be stolen out of the man's house; if the thief be found, let him pay double. If the thief be not found, then the master of the *house shall be brought unto the judges, to see whether he have put his hand unto his neighbour's goods. For all manner of trespass, whether it be for ox, for ass, for sheep, for raiment, or for any manner of lost thing, which another challengeth to be his, the cause of both parties shall come before the judges; and whom the judges shall condemn, he shall pay double unto his neighbour. If a man deliver unto his neighbour an ass, or an ox, or a sheep, or any beast, to keep; and it die, or be hurt, or driven away, no man seeing it:...And if it be stolen from him, he shall make restitution unto the owner thereof."*

Exodus 22:1,4-10, 12

Also, the Bible in the book of Proverbs says,

*Men do not despise a thief, if he steal to satisfy his soul when he is hungry; But if he be found, he shall restore sevenfold; he shall give all the*

*substance of his house.*

Proverbs 6:30-31.

*"And the LORD spake unto Moses,*

*saying, If a soul sin, and commit a*

*trespass against the LORD, and lie*

*unto his neighbour in that which was*

*delivered him to keep, or in*

*fellowship, or in a thing taken away*

*by violence, or hath deceived his*

*neighbour; Or have found that which*

*was lost, and lieth concerning it, and*

*sweareth falsely; in any of all these that a man doeth, sinning therein: then it shall be, because he hath sinned, and is guilty, that he shall restore that which he took violently away, or the thing which he hath deceitfully gotten, or that which was delivered him to keep, or the lost thing which he found then it shall be, because he hath sinned, and is guilty, that he shall restore that which he took violently away, or the thing which he hath deceitfully gotten, or that which was delivered him to keep, or the lost thing which he found or all that about which he hath sworn falsely; he shall even restore it in the principal, and shall add the fifth part more thereto, and give it unto him to whom it appertaineth, in the day of his trespass offering.*

Leviticus 6:1-5

We must understand that the devil can't steal from us except we give him an opportunity to. This the devil does when we have these characteristics as New Creations - Ignorant, Unarmed, and Asleep.

The devil has stolen so much from a believer in the past because he was all or some of the characteristics (that is, Ignorant, Unarmed, and Asleep).

As children of God, if we want the devil to restore all he stole from us then, we must do the following;

1.  Know the truth.

   *"and ye shall know the truth, and the truth shall make you free."*

   John 8:32.

2.  Put on the whole armor of God.

   *"Put on the whole armour of God, that ye may be able to stand against the wiles of the devil. For we wrestle not against flesh and blood, but against principalities, against powers,*

against the rulers of the darkness of this world, against spiritual wickedness in high places. Wherefore take unto you the whole armour of God, that ye may be able to withstand in the evil day, and having done all, to stand. Stand therefore, having your loins girt about with truth, and having on the breastplate of righteousness; and your feet shod with the preparation of the gospel of peace; above all, taking the shield of faith, wherewith ye shall be able to quench all the fiery darts of the *wicked. And take the helmet of salvation, and the sword of the Spirit, which is the word of God: praying always with all prayer and supplication in the Spirit, and watching thereunto with all perseverance and supplication for all saints;"*

Ephesians 6:11-18.

3.  Watch and pray.

*Watch and pray, that ye enter not into temptation: the spirit indeed is willing, but the flesh is weak.*

Matthew 26:41.

YOU CAN HAVE IT ALL.

# THE TRUTH TO KNOW

Christ Jesus said in the book of

John chapter 10 verse 10b,

" *...I am come that ye may have life*

*and have it more abundantly*".

Page 138

Also, Jesus said in the book of John chapter 14 verse 6,

*"I am the way, the truth and the life"*.

In addition, in the book of 1 John chapter 3:8b the Bible says,

*"For this purpose the son of God was manifested, that he might destroy the works of the devil."*

Therefore, Jesus is the one who came to give life in exchange for death and destruction. Because death and destruction are the major provisions of the devil.

By giving life, Christ Jesus destroyed the works of the devil. We can only receive the life Jesus gives when we receive Him, His finished work for us, and His intercessory work for us.

Hence, the Person, Purpose (that is, Finished work), Position, and profession (that is, the intercessory work of Jesus before The Father) is THE TRUTH.

YOU CAN HAVE IT ALL.

# HOW IS A THIEF TO RESTITUTE?

The Bible in the book of Exodus 22 reveals how God tells a thief to restitute for items stolen. God instructed saying;

- Five (5) Oxen for one (1) Ox.

- Four (4) Sheep for one (1) Sheep.

*"If a man shall steal an ox, or a sheep, and kill it, or sell it; he shall restore five oxen for an ox, and four sheep for a sheep."*

Exodus 22:1

According to verse 4 of the book of Exodus chapter 22, God tells how a thief is to restitute two (2) folds (that

is, double) for items stolen if it is
found alive in his hands.


*"If the theft be certainly found in his
hand alive, whether it be ox, or ass, or
sheep; he shall restore double"*.

Exodus 22:4


In the book of Exodus chapter
22, God tells how a man who allows for
another man's farm/field to be grazed
or releases his livestock to graze on the

said field, the thief is to restitute with the best crop of his own field/farm.

*"If a man shall cause a field or vineyard to be eaten, and shall put in his beast, and shall feed in another man's field; of the best of his own field, and of the best of his own vineyard, shall he make restitution."*

Exodus 22:5

In the book of Exodus chapter 22, God tells how a thief, who breaks into someone's house and steals money. The thief is to restitute double for the money stolen.

*"If a man shall deliver unto his neighbour money or stuff to keep, and it be stolen out of the man's house; if the thief be found, let him pay double. If the thief be not found, then the master of the house shall be brought unto the judges, to see whether he*

*have put his hand unto his*

*neighbour's goods."*

Exodus 22:7-8

Furthermore in the book of

Exodus 22, God tells how a thief is to

restitute for all manner of items stolen,

it is double fold.

*"For all manner of trespass, whether*

*it be for ox, for ass, for sheep, for*

*raiment, or for any manner of lost*

*thing, which another challengeth to be his, the cause of both parties shall come before the judges; and whom the judges shall condemn, he shall pay double unto his neighbour."*

Exodus 22:9

More so, in the book of Leviticus chapter 6, God tells how a thief who stole to satisfy his soul is to return when he is caught, it is the principal and a fifth portion i.e 120%.

*"or all that about which he hath worn falsely; he shall even restore it in the principal, and shall add the fifth part more thereto, and give it unto him to whom it appertaineth, in the day of his trespass offering."*

Leviticus 6:5

In the book of Proverbs chapter 6, God tells how a thief who steals by falsehood or deception is to return when he is caught, it is seven-fold.

*"Men do not despise a thief, if he steal to satisfy his soul when he is hungry; But if he be found, he shall restore sevenfold; He shall give all the substance of his house."*

Proverbs 6:30-31.

Therefore, per the above scriptures, the devil is to restitute the believer he has stolen from in the following ways:

1. Five times more for everything you use to work and get a livelihood which he stole from you.

2. Four times more of your products, goods, and services which he stole from you.

3. Two times for items he stole from you if it is found alive in his hands.

4. His best for consuming the fruit of your labor.

5. One hundred and twenty percent, if he stole it to satisfy himself.

6. Seven times more if he stole it by deception or falsehood.

YOU CAN HAVE IT ALL.

# HOW TO MAKE THE

# DEVIL RESTITUTE

Following the scriptures under

consideration, the believer is

empowered to make the devil restitute

all that has been stolen in the following ways;

1. Catch the devil in His act. To catch the devil in his act it can only be through revelation.

*"and ye shall know the truth, and the truth shall make you free."*

John 8:32

2. Bring the devil to the judge of all that is, God in prayers.

*"Produce your cause, saith the LORD;*

*bring forth your strong reasons, saith*

*the King of Jacob."*

Isaiah 41:21

3. Execute the judgment of God on the devil.

*"Let the high praises of God be in their*

*mouth, And a twoedged sword in their*

*hand; To execute vengeance upon the*

*heathen, And punishments upon the*

*people; To bind their kings with chains, And their nobles with fetters of iron; To execute upon them the judgment written: This honour have all his saints. Praise ye the LORD."*

Psalms 149: 6-9.

## The Truth About The Finished Work Of Jesus.

Because of the finished work of Jesus, the devil has no right to steal from you again. And, the devil has no right to condemn you before God when you sin.

*"There is therefore now no condemnation to them which are in Christ Jesus, who walk not after the flesh, but after the Spirit".*

Romans 8:1

This is because God has made you the righteousness of God in Christ.

*"For he hath made him to be sin for us, who knew no sin; that we might be made the righteousness of God in him"*.

2 Corinthians 5:21.

This means that every believer has all authority and right to command the devil to return all the devil stole. (Proverbs 6:30-31). The devil is to restore to the believer seven (7) times as much as what he has stolen.

Consider the Bible accounts cited below, it is the story of Job that aids our understanding of the restoration of all the devil has stolen as well as, best explaining the seven-fold restoration.

Here is a summary of the ordeal of Job of the devil's stealing escapades in his life and family.

1.  The devil stole Job's animals and servants.

*"and there came a messenger unto Job, and said, The oxen were plowing, and the asses feeding beside them: and the Sabeans fell upon them, and took them away; yea, they have slain the servants with the edge of the sword; and I only am escaped alone to tell thee."*

Job 1:14-15

*"While he was yet speaking, there came also another, and said, The fire of God is fallen from heaven, and hath burned up the sheep, and the servants, and consumed them; and I only am escaped alone to tell thee."*

Job 1:16

*"While he was yet speaking, there came also another, and said, The Chaldeans made out three bands, and fell upon the camels, and have carried them away, yea, and slain the*

*servants with the edge of the sword;*

*and I only am escaped alone to tell*

*thee."*

Job 1:17.

2.  The devil stole Job's son and
daughters.

*"While he was yet speaking, there*

*came also another, and said, Thy sons*

*and thy daughters were eating and*

*drinking wine in their eldest brother's*

*house: and, behold, there came a*

*great wind from the wilderness, and*

*smote the four corners of the house,*

*and it fell upon the young men, and*

*they are dead; and I only am escaped*

*alone to tell thee."*

Job 1:18-19.

3. The devil stole Job's health and gives him boils.

*"So went Satan forth from the*

*presence of the LORD, and smote Job*

*with sore boils from the sole of his foot*

*unto his crown."*

Job 2:7

In the end, regarding the latter

end of Job, the scripture reveals,

*"So the LORD blessed the latter end of*

*Job more than his beginning: for he*

*had fourteen thousand sheep, and six*

*thousand camels, and a thousand*

*yoke of oxen, and a thousand she*

asses. He had also seven sons and three daughters. And he called the name of the first, Jemima; and the name of the second, Kezia; and the name of the third, Keren-happuch. And in all the land were no women found so fair as the daughters of Job: and their father gave them inheritance among their brethren. After this lived Job an hundred and forty years, and saw his sons, and his sons' sons, even four generations. So Job died, being old and full of days."

Job 42:12-17.

The devil returns seven-fold by stopping his stealing operation at our command and giving way for God to restore us seven times more. The devil is to restore to us his entire household.

Concerning Joseph, the scripture reveals that the devil stole so much from Joseph in thirteen (13) years, but in one day, God made Joseph a prime minister, and an economic adviser.

Also, Joseph was given a presidential house, and in a moment made a presidential car (chariot) owner. Joseph became the son-in-law of one of the renowned priests in Egypt.

*"And Pharaoh said unto Joseph, See, I have set thee over all the land of*

Egypt. And Pharaoh took off his ring from his hand, and put it upon Joseph's hand, and arrayed him in vestures of fine linen, and put a gold chain about his neck; and he made him to ride in the second chariot which he had; and they cried before him, Bow the knee: and he made him ruler over all the land of Egypt. And Pharaoh said unto Joseph, I am Pharaoh, and without thee shall no man lift up his hand or foot in all the land of Egypt. And Pharaoh called Joseph's name Zaphnath-paaneah;

*and he gave him to wife Asenath the daughter of Poti-pherah priest of On. And Joseph went out over all the land of Egypt."*

Genesis 41:39-45.


Bible dictionary reveals that On is a city in lower Egypt in Joseph's days, a city bordering the land of Goshen, the city Pharaoh later assigned to Joseph for his father and brethren.

"Then Joseph came and told Pharaoh, and said, My father and my brethren, and their flocks, and their herds, and all that they have, are come out of the land of Canaan; and, behold, they are in the land of Goshen. And he took some of his brethren, even five men, and presented them unto Pharaoh. And Pharaoh said unto his brethren, What is your occupation? And they said unto Pharaoh, Thy servants are shepherds, both we, and also our fathers. They said moreover unto Pharaoh, For to sojourn in the land are we come; for thy servants have no pasture for their flocks; for the famine is sore in the land of Canaan: now therefore, we pray thee, let thy servants dwell in the land of Goshen. And Pharaoh spake unto Joseph, saying, Thy father and thy brethren are come unto thee: the land of Egypt is before thee; in the best of the land make thy father and brethren to dwell; in the land of Goshen let them dwell: and if thou knowest any men of *activity among them, then make them*

*rulers over my cattle."*

Genesis 47:1-6.

So, Jacob and Joseph's brethren benefited from the restoration package too, as they were supernaturally assigned the best of the land of Egypt by Pharaoh.

Also, according to the account in the book of Leviticus chapter 6 stated below, the devil is to restore one hundred and twenty percent ( 120%) of all he stole from the child of God in the past.

*"And the LORD spake unto Moses, saying, If a soul sin, and commit a trespass against the LORD, and lie unto his neighbour in that which was delivered him to keep, or in fellowship, or in a thing taken away by violence, or hath deceived his neighbour; or have found that which*

was lost, and lieth concerning it, and

sweareth falsely; in any of all these

that a man doeth, sinning therein:

then it shall be, because he hath

sinned, and is guilty, that he shall

restore that which he took violently

away, or the thing which he hath

deceitfully gotten, or that which was

delivered him to keep, or the lost thing

which he found, or all that about

which he hath sworn falsely; he shall

even restore it in the principal, and

shall add the fifth part more thereto,

and give it unto him to whom it

*appertaineth, in the day of his*

*trespass offering."*

Leviticus 6:1-5.

# ACTION / PRAYER POINT

Job prayed for his friends after which, God restored him. Decide today to pray for someone else you know that the devil has stolen the same thing he stole from you (Job 42:12).

- Declare saying, "Satan I command you in the name of Jesus, beginning from now restore seven times more than all

you stole from me from my birth day
till date."


- Declare saying, "Satan I command you
  in the name of Jesus, beginning from
  now restore one hundred and twenty
  percent (120%) of all you stole from me
  from my birth day till now."

# JESUS IS LORD.

# OTHER BOOKS BY CHIMDI OHAHUNA MINISTRY INTERNATIONAL.

1. **LIGHTEN UP.** By Chimdi Ohahuna.

2. **I WANT TO KNOW THE HOLY SPIRIT (prepared as WORKBOOK).** Volume 1 By Chimdi and Funke Ohahuna.

3. **A JOURNEY THROUGH THE WILDERNESS.** By Funke Ohahuna.

**4. THE GREATEST WORD FROM THE GREATEST MAN.** By Chimdi Ohahuna.

**5. Hello Beloved, GET MOVING.** By Chimdi Ohahuna.

**6. ACCESSING AND HARNESSING UNSEARCHABLE RICHES** Book Series. By Chimdi & Funke Ohahuna.

Series 1- **THE MONEY IN YOU.**

Series 2- **MONEY SHADES.**

Purchase soft and hard copies online via Amazon.

Or, write the ministry for hardcopy purchase via:

chimdiohahunaministry@gmail.com

For additional information on Chimdi Ohahuna Teachings and resources;

**Website:**

www.chimdiohahunaministry.org

**Podcast: GRACELIFECOMI**

https://anchor.fm/chimdi-ohahuna

**Email:**

chimdiohahunaministry@gmail.com